5-7-5

The Haiku of Issa

The Buddhist Society Trust is a distinguished press in the United Kingdom which enriches lives around the world by advancing the study and practice of Buddhism.

Its activities are supported by charitable contributions from individuals and institutions.

For more information visit: info@thebuddhistsociety.org

First published by The Buddhist Society Trust, 2019

The Buddhist Society Trust
E: middlewayandpublishing@gmail.com

ISBN: 978-0-901032-58-4
(The Buddhist Society Trust)

A catalogue record for this book is available from the British Library

Designed by Avni Patel
Technical assistance by Kenshin Hiroshi Ishii

Printed and bound in Wales by Gomer Press

5–7–5

The Haiku of Issa

John White & Kemmyo Taira Sato

THE BUDDHIST SOCIETY TRUST

FRONTISPIECE
From the woodblock version of *The Oragaharu* by Issa,
Issa Memorial Hall.

Contents

Introduction

OF THE GREAT TRIUMVIRATE of Japanese haiku poets, Matsuo Basho (1644–1694), Yosa Buson (1716–1783) and Kobayashi Issa (1763–1828), whose lifetimes span the better part of two hundred years, it is perhaps Issa who is the most paradoxical.

The paradox lies in the fact that, on the one hand, as a devout Shin Buddhist, he was thoroughly conservative in doctrinal terms, while in his poetry he was far more colloquial and down to earth than were his predecessors.

Though Basho's Buddhism was in the very air he breathed and it pervades his poetry, he was completely non-sectarian in outlook and on his travels seems to have visited and prayed in as many Shinto shrines as Buddhist temples.

In contrast, Issa's Buddhism is openly displayed in haiku after haiku in a lifetime catalogue running to some twenty thousand items.

Shin Buddhism is in the foreground, not the background, of his work. It goes without saying that in this vast output not every haiku reaches the very highest peaks of his endeavour and there is a good deal of repetition and near repetition, of returning to, and of reworking, an idea in content and in wording alike in a constant struggle for perfection.

Nevertheless, his haiku, in the seemingly endless variety of their approach to his chosen themes, and in their sensitivity and sudden, unexpected insights, are more fun and more approachable than might be expected in such a tightly controlled and constricted form of poetry, but to underrate him because of this is a mistake, for he can on occasion be profound in the extreme.

There has, perhaps, never been a better symbol or encapsulation of the content of the whole vast literature of the sutras than the first five syllables of haiku no. 137, which begins 'on a lotus leaf' and then goes on to say that, seen in this light, all the dewdrops of this world, which time and again he uses as a symbol of perfection, are themselves misshapen or distorted.

Not only are they prime exemplars of the evanescence, the impermanence, of all created things, but a sharp reminder of the Buddhist realisation that, in this world, all is illusion.

Indeed, one major feature, which frequently distinguishes a great haiku from good one, is its ability in seventeen syllables to open up a host of different ideas.

This faces translators, in their turn, with the problem, in such cases, of not closing down their potential by focussing those few syllables on a single possible meaning, but of keeping open as many options as possible.

Another prime example in Issa's case is haiku no. 146 in this collection, which shows how he, though different in so many ways, was like Basho before him able to use some simple, detailed happening in the day-to-day world to make the seventeen syllables of a haiku suddenly take in the universe.

On a more technical note, there is the fact that quite apart from the vastly different cultural background and linguistic structure of Japanese and English, there are such minor oddities as the fact that the letter 'n', when it is not succeeded by a vowel, and likewise any doubled consonant, counts as a single sound-bite on its own, or an added syllable in its English counterpart.

As a result the translator has, in some ways, a more difficult task than with his predecessors because of what seems on the surface to be a more easy-going and colloquial approach.

These difficulties are, of course, greatly increased by the decision, as with an earlier translation of three hundred of Basho's haiku, to follow the essential, 5–7–5 format of the originals with unremitting strictness.

Only then can the resulting poem properly be called a haiku, though that term is freely used of almost any short, derivative piece of poetry. In terms of content, there is also every attempt, with very few exceptions, to maintain the line by line sequences which play so important a role in the Japanese originals.

Historically speaking, poetry is essentially a rhythmic form of speech and this perhaps presents by far the greatest difficulty facing a translator who is trying to come as close as possible, not only to the form, but to the spirit of what was actually written.

Despite its brevity of format, rhythm lies at the very heart of haiku, and to expand or to contract its sound-bite or syllabic structure to any great extent is to lose all hope of finding a rhythmic counterpart in another language.

In terms of general organisation, the present work is once more set out season by season in a four year cycle, honouring the strict catalogue of seasonal marker words created to control the actual placement of each haiku, quite often seemingly regardless of the actual facts observable in nature.

The intervening illustrations further emphasise the fact that in Issa's day, and in the world of haiku in particular, the seasons did not flow haphazardly along, but changed quite sharply on specifically designated days.

To say that Issa was conservative as far as his fundamental religious faith was concerned is no exaggeration.

Reincarnation lay at the very heart of his beliefs, which is much less the case for many modern Buddhists and for western, English speaking Buddhists in particular.

For him, a mountain cuckoo might have been his cousin in a former life and he could rest in the cool shade of a tree with a butterfly which had, in a previous existence, been his friend, or hope that in his next life he himself could be one, flying free, though he well knew that he and they, for all their seeming, carefree beauty, were no more than dust.

Such haiku, with their implication that the process of reincarnation was, for him by no means over, are a warning that even in the case of a poet such as Issa, it would be a great mistake to apply too rigid and restrictive a doctrinal or sectarian label to the nature of his personal beliefs and ways of looking at the world.

He, of course, could talk to insects as he did to people, caring for their welfare, fleas and all, including those who lived with him, enjoining them, as he was going out, to go on practising their jumping in spite of the cramped nature of the living space they shared.

For children it is wholly natural to talk to animals and insects and endow them with all kinds of human attributes and feelings, but Issa's thoroughgoing anthropomorphism was something deeper than mere childishness.

Along with the impermanence of all existing things, and his own sharp awareness of the imminence of death, it is an accompaniment of another basic Buddhist concept, that of emptiness, the lack of any lasting self or soul.

It is a way of bringing down to earth and giving actuality, through his references to the most humble forms of everyday life, to what appears at times to be the rather abstract Buddhist belief in the unity of all that is and that is not.

And down to earth indeed he is.

His constant talk of fleas and flies and lice, of the intensity of winter cold and of the overpowering, sweaty heat of summers swarming with mosquitoes; his references in poetry to farting, to the dung of animals and its attractions, and to human defecation, brings home, as no leading English poet ever did, the actualities of eighteenth century life.

Yet, in haiku after haiku, he ventures far beyond the majority of his co-religionists, in seeing every living thing as Buddha.

The Pure Land in the west, so far beyond the sunset, is indeed within.

A dewdrop in the instant that it vanishes, a pine tree or a flower as it dies, a flea, a skylark or a prostitute, is Buddha.

This unity embraces not just the external world, but also our five senses, with results that call to mind the modern clinical condition, known as synaesthesia, in which an input into any one sense is instantly accompanied by involuntary experiences in another.

In Issa's haiku, instances of this are not as common as they are in those of Basho, but when they do occur can be extreme, as when the song of a living cicada and the sound made by an inorganic paper windmill are both seen as being red.

Issa's concern and his compassion for every aspect of the natural world, was extended, with occasional exceptions, to the people who surrounded him, and given added poignancy by his own life experiences.

Born a farmer's son in a small mountain village, his mother died when he was only three, and since the woman that his father subsequently married thoroughly mistreated him, he was cared for by his grandmother, who herself died when he was just fourteen, and in the following year, because of the unending family discord, his father suddenly packed him off to distant Edo, which was then the capital of Japan and where he was instantaneously scorned as being just one more impoverished, migrant peasant.

After a decade, he became a student in a school of haiku, but after just a single year he set out to become a self-styled, roving and impoverished poet-priest in search of inspiration.

In their own way, his constant journeyings matched those of Basho, long before him.

Three years after he had died, his erstwhile students put up a stone monument with engraved on it a haiku, which referred to his travelling through some sixty provinces.

When at length in 1810, he did return to his home village, he was still rejected by his family, and it was only after years of litigation that the farmhouse was divided into two and one half was allotted to him in what had in the past been such a miserable home.

There he married Kiku, only for his misery and loneliness to be compounded by the early death of his four children, swiftly followed by that of Kiku herself.

His poverty and his feeling for the orphaned and the poor, his sense of the injustice and depravity of the world in which he lived, together with his sensitivity to the passage of the seasons and the beauties they engendered, were with him all his life, as were his irony and his sense of humour and self-deprecation.

There is, it seems, no way to sum up such a life except, perhaps, by picking on some simple, gentle, child-endearing thing, as when he said, with the approach of winter,

katatsuburi
ware to kite sume
hatsu shigure

come on in you snail
and live together with me
in winter's first rain

The Haiku

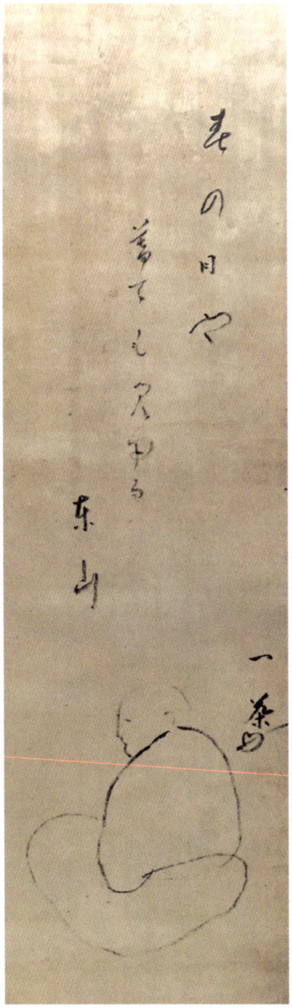

PLATE 1
Drawing and calligraphy by Issa,
Kobayashi Issa Museum. See haiku 1.

1.

春の日や暮ても見ゆる東山

haru no hi ya
kure te mo miyuru
higashiyama

in the springtime day
after sunset you still see
higashiyama

*1

2.

小島にも畠打也鳴雲雀

kojima ni mo
hatake utsu nari
naku hibari

even small islands
have men preparing the fields
and skylarks in song

3.

鳥の音に咲うともせず藪の梅

tori no ne ni
sakō to mo se zu
yabu no ume

the birds are singing
yet the plum trees aren't ready
to bloom in the grove

4.

菜のはなの中を浅间のけぶり哉

nanohana no
naka o asama no
keburi kana

in amongst the rape
flowers there is to be seen
mount asama's smoke

*2

5.

寝ておわしても仏ぞよ花が降る

nete owashi temo
hotoke zo yo
hana ga furu

although he is sleeping now
he is the buddha
and flowers rain down

6.

寝て起て大欠して猫の恋

nete okite
ōakubi shite
neko no koi

getting up from sleep
with enormous yawns, the cat
goes out to make love

7.

蝶とぶや此世に望みないやうに

chō tobu ya
kono yo ni nozomi
nai yō ni

a butterfly flies
as if wishing for nothing
that's here in this world

8.

むつましや生れかはらばのべの蝶

mutsumashi ya
umare kawara ba
nobe no chō

how happy they are!
i wish i could be reborn
a field butterfly

9.

萩の葉に鹿のくれけり春の雨

hagi no ha ni
hika no kure keri
haru no ame

amid bush clovers
there is a deer hiding out
in the springtime rain

10.

観音のあらんかぎりは桜かな

kannon no
ara n kagiri wa
sakura kana

wherever kannon
is found, there will also be
cherry tree blossoms

*3

11.

夜ざくらや美人天から下るとも

yozakura ya
bijin ten kara
kudaru tomo

night cherry blossoms,
lovely ladies from heaven
come down it is said

12.

花の陰赤の他人はなかりけり

hana no kage
aka no tanin wa
nakari keri

under cherry tree
blossoms no one can ever
be total strangers

13.

貧乏人花見ぬ春はなかりけり

binbōnin
hana mi nu haru wa
nakari keri

for the poor people
springtime never arrives
without its blossoms

14.

大名を馬からおろす桜哉

daimyō o
uma kara orosu
sakura kana

even lords are forced
to dismount from their horses
by cherry blossom

15.

鶯や御前へ出ても同じ声

uguisu ya
gozen e dete mo
onaji koe

the bush warblers when
in the presence of nobles
sing just the same song

16.

春風や牛に引かれて善光寺

harukaze ya
ushi ni hikarete
zenkōji

in the springtime breeze
the cow is leading the way
up to zenkoji

*4

17.

雀子も梅に口明く念仏哉

suzumego mo
ume ni kuchi aku
nebutsu kana

for young sparrows too,
open-mouthed at plum blossoms
that's nenbutsu

*5

18.

つるべにも一夜過ぎけりなく蛙

tsurube ni mo
hito yo sugi keri
naku kawazu

in the well bucket
even, it croaks the whole night
the frog that is there

19.

痩蛙まけるな一茶是にあり

yase gaeru
makeru na issa
kore ni ari

you skinny frog there,
now that issa is here you
must fight for dear life

20.

松の木に蛙も見るや宮角力

matsu no ki ni
kawazu mo miru ya
miya-zumō

from among the pines
the frogs too watch the sumo
held there at the shrine

PLATE 2
Drawing by Matsumoto Hōji,
Osaka Museum of History.

21.

五月雨の竹にはさまる在所哉

samidare no
take ni hasamaru
zaisho kana

in the summer rains,
squeezed in amongst the bamboos,
my native village

*6

22.

藪むらや貧乏馴れて夕すゞみ

yabu-mura ya
binbō narete
yūsuzumi

in a poor hamlet
accustomed to poverty
evening coolness

23.

涼風の窓が極楽浄土哉

suzukaze no
mado ga gokuraku
jōdo kana

the breeze's coolness
acts as a window onto
the pure land of bliss

*7

24.

飯けぶり聳る里やほとゝぎす

meshi keburi
sobiyuru sato ya
hototogisu

the rice cooking smoke
rises over the hamlet,
the call of a cuckoo

25.

世がよくばもう一つ留れ飯の蝿

yo ga yoku ba
mo hitotsu tomare
meshi no hae

as all now goes well
with the world let another
fly onto the rice

26.

はつ蛍其手はくはぬとびぶりや

hatsu hotaru
sono te wa kuwa nu
tobi buri ya

the first firefly, as
it was avoiding my hand,
flew in just that way

27.

蟻の道雲の峰よりつゞきけん

ari no michi
kumo no mine yori
tsuzuki ken

this pathway for ants,
it is from the cloud mountains
it seems to emerge

28.

ちょんぼりと不二の小脇の柳哉

chonbori to
fuji no kowaki no
yanagi kana

a minuscule thing
at the side of mount fuji
is a willow tree

29.

芝の戸や錠のかはりに蝸牛

shiba no to ya
jō no kawari ni
katatsumuri

for a brushwood gate
that's in need of a lock now
this snail is enough

30.

我宿は口で吹ても出る蚊哉

waga yado wa
kuchi de fui temo
deru ka kana

here in my cottage,
although i blow them away
mosquitoes come out

31.

逃るなり紙魚が中にも親よ子よ

nigeru nari
shimi ga naka ni mo
oya yo ko yo

as they run away
those silverfish there are both
parents and children

32.

蚤噛んだ口でなむあみだ仏哉

nomi kan da
kuchi de namuami
dabutsu kana

when cracking a flea
it's the mouth that said namu
amida butsu

*8

33.

宵越しの豆腐明りに藪蚊かな

yoigoshi no
tōfu akari ni
yabuka kana

tofu makers' lights
shine throughout the night, and striped
mosquitoes hover

34.

蚤どもが夜永だらうぞ淋しかろ

nomi domo ga
yonaga darō zo
sabishikaro

for all of you fleas
the night may prove to be long
and be lonely too

35.

涼しさは雲の大峰小みね哉

suzushisa wa
kumo no ō-mine
ko-mine kana

how cool it now is;
the clouds with their great summits
above smaller peaks

36.

おのずから頭が下る也神ぢ山

onozukara
zu ga sagaru nari
kamijiyama

of its own accord
my head's bowing down so low
to mount kamiji

*9

37.

とぶな蚤それ〳〵そこが角田川

tobu na nomi
sore sore soko ga
sumidagawa

flea, don't ever jump
over that way for there lies
river sumida

*10

38.

手伝て虱を拾へ雀の子

tetsudatte
shirami o hiroe
suzume no ko

i need to have help
in picking off all these lice,
you little sparrow

39.

松のせみどこ迄鳴て昼になる

matsu no semi
doko made naite
hiru ni naru

pine tree cicadas
how long do you have to sing
for it to be noon

40.

松散や茸の時は誰かある

matsu chiru ya
kinoko no toki wa
dare ka aru

pines shed their needles;
when mushroom hunting time comes
who will then be here

41.

身の上の鐘ともしらで夕涼

mi no ue no
kane to mo shira de
yūsuzumi

unaware the bell
is tolling my life away
in evening cool

42.

涼風の出口もいくつ松かしは

suzukaze no
deguchi mo ikutsu
matsu kashiwa

how many gateways
for the cool breezes to blow
through pine trees and oaks

43.

入相の鐘にちらばふ鵜舟哉

iriai no
kane ni chirabō
ubune kana

the setting sun bell
is the time of dispersal
for cormorant boats

44.

雨三粒天から土用見舞かな

ame mi tsubu
ten kara doyō
mimai kana

just three drops of rain
are a greeting from heaven
in midsummer heat

45.

更衣しばししらみを忘れたり

koromogae
shibashi shirami o
wasure tari

a new summer robe
and so for a little while
fleas are forgotten

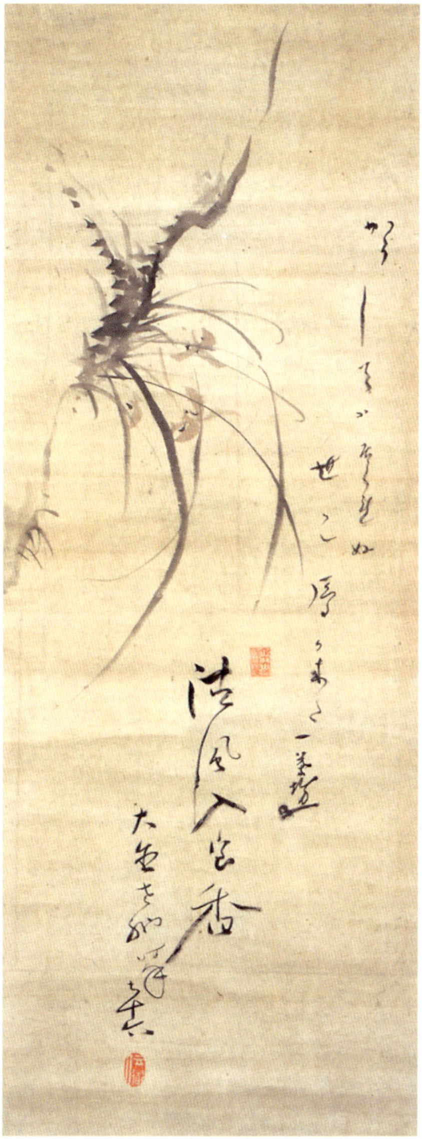

PLATE 3
Drawing by Ōu Sanō, calligraphy by Issa,
Issa Memorial Hall. See haiku 46.

46. かうしては居られぬ世也雁が来た

kōshite wa
orare nu yo nari
kari ga ki ta

to live here like this
is not allowed now that
the geese have arrived

47.

雁よ雁いくつのとしから旅をした

kari yo kari
ikutsu no toshi kara
tabi o shi ta

wild goose, wild goose there,
how old were you when you set out
on that first journey

48.

帰雁浅间のけぶりいく度見る

kaeru kari
asama no keburi
ikudo miru

wild geese on your way
you've seen mount asama's smoke
how many times now

*11

49.

遠山が目玉にうつるとんぼ哉

tōyama ga
medama ni utsuru
tonbo kana

the distant mountains
reflect themselves in the eye
of a dragonfly

50.

秋風やむしりたがりし赤い花

akikaze ya
mushiri tagari shi
akai hana

in the autumn breeze
are scarlet flowers that she
would have liked to pick

*12

51.

なかくに人と生れて秋の暮

naka naka ni
hito to umarete
aki no kure

unknowingly i
have been born as a human,
twilight in autumn

52.

秋のてふかゞしの袖にすがりけり

aki no chō
kagashi no sode ni
sugari keri

autumn butterfly
on the sleeve of a scarecrow
is clinging to it

53.

石仏誰が持たせし草の花

ishibotoke
tare ga motase shi
kusa no hana

buddha carved in stone,
who is it garlanded you
with the wildflowers

54.

御祭の赤い出立の蜻蛉哉

omatsuri no
akai dedachi no
tonbo kana

to the festival
all dressed up in their red clothes
go the dragonflies

55.

出て行ぞ仲よく遊べきりぎくす

dete iku zo
naka yoku asobe
kirigirisu

as i'm going out,
play now in a friendly way
all you crickets there

56.

小便の香も通ひけり菊の花

shōben no
ka mo kayoi keri
kiku no hana

a smell of urine
was drifting along among
chrysanthemum blooms

57.

大名と肩並べけりきくの花

daimyō to
kata narabe keri
kiku no hana

the lord of the land
is not any taller than
a chrysanthemum

58.

けさ程やこそりとおちてある一葉

kesa hodo ya
kosori to ochite
aru hitoha

it was this morning
that one leaf quietly fell
from the empress tree

59.

夕晴や浅黄に並ぶ秋の山

yūbare ya
asagi ni narabu
aki no yama

the evening clears
and seen in their pale yellows
are autumn mountains

60.

名月や山有川有寝ながらに

meigetsu ya
yama ari kawa ari
ne nagara ni

the harvest moon shines
over mountains and rivers
while i am asleep

61.

代々の貧乏垣の木槿哉

daidai no
binbō-gaki no
mukuge kana

for generations
in this meagre fence have been
roses of sharon

62.

大切に仕廻て置しかがしかな

taisetsu ni
shimatte oki shi
kagashi kana

put into storage
as something of great value,
it is a scarecrow

63.

古犬が先に立也はか参り

furu-inu ga
saki ni tatsu nari
haka-mairi

it is the old dog
that is always the leader
when visiting graves

64.

露ちるや後生大事に鳴雀

tsuyu chiru ya
goshō daiji ni
naku suzume

dewdrops scattering;
next birth is the great concern
of the sparrows' song

65.

墨染の蝶が飛なり秋の風

sumizome no
chō ga tobu nari
aki no kaze

clothed in its black robe
there's a butterfly flying
in the autumn wind

*13

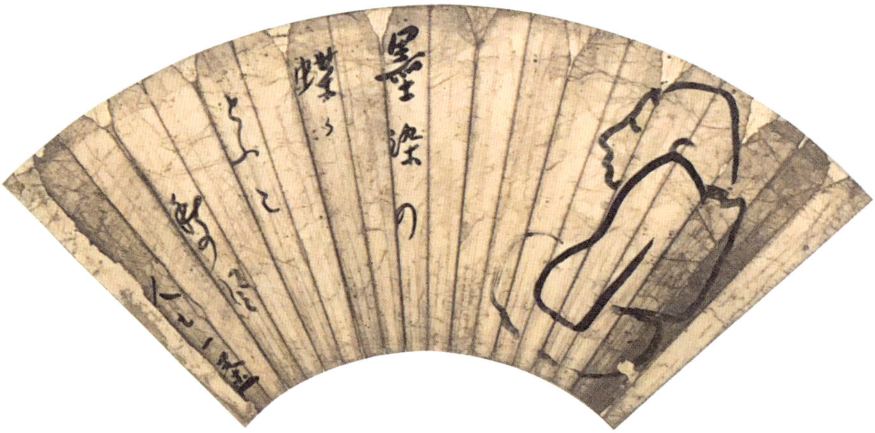

PLATE 4
Drawing and Calligraphy by Issa,
Kobayashi Issa Museum. See haiku 65.

66.

茶の花に隠んぼする雀哉

cha no hana ni
kakurenbo suru
suzume kana

among tea flowers
hide-and-seek, that is the game
that the sparrows play

67.

月さして千鳥に埋る笹家哉

tsuki sashite
chidori ni umaru
sasaya kana

under the moonlight
the plovers cover the roof
of my small, thatched house

68.

重箱の銭四五文や夕時雨

jūbako no
zeni shi go mon ya
yū shigure

in a beggar's box
no more than four or five pence;
rainy winter night

69.

掃溜も鶴だらけ也和歌の浦

hakidame mo
tsuru darake nari
wakanoura

on the rubbish pile
there's only a swarm of cranes;
wakanoura!

*14

70.

冬籠其夜に聞くや山の雨

fuyugomori
sono yo ni kiku ya
yama no ame

winter seclusion;
i listened that evening
to the mountain rain

71. 山寺や木がらしの上に寝るがごと

yamadera ya
kogarashi no ue ni
neru ga goto

the mountain temple
appears to be taking a nap
on the winter wind

72.

大寒や八月ほしき松の月

daikan ya
hachigatsu hoshiki
matsu no tsuki

the time of great cold,
i wish it were september;
moonlight in pine trees

73.

野仏の御鼻の先の氷柱かな

nobotoke no
ohana no saki no
tsurara kana

from the very tip
of a rural buddha's nose
an icicle hangs

74.

門口に来て氷也三井の鐘

kadoguchi ni
kite kōru nari
mii no kane

on reaching the gate
it began to be frozen,
miidera's bell

*15

75.

次の間の灯で膳につく寒さ哉

tsugi no ma no
hi de zen ni tsuku
samusa kana

in the next room's light
i sit at my small table,
how chilly it is

76.

霜がれや鍋の炭かく小傾城

shimogare ya
nabe no sumi kaku
ko-keisei

in withering frost
a young harlot is scraping
soot from a saucepan

*16

77.

もろ〱の愚者も月夜の十夜哉

moromoro no
gusha mo tsukiyo no
jūya kana

with lots of fools too
on a moonlit evening
the ten night retreat

*17

78.

雲と見し桜は炭にやかれけり

kumo to mi shi
sakura wa sumi ni
yakare keri

once seen as a cloud
of blossom a cherry tree
burned into charcoal

79.

笠でするさらば〳〵や薄がすみ

kasa de suru
saraba saraba ya
usu gasumi

as i raise my hat
it's to say goodbye goodbye
to the springtime mist

*18

PLATE 5
Drawing and calligraphy by Issa,
Issa Memorial Hall. See haiku 79.

80.

春立や愚の上に又愚にかへる

haru tatsu ya
gu no ue ni mata
gu ni kaeru

the spring has begun
and ignorance just becomes
ignorance once more

81.

弥陀仏の見ておはす也ちる桜

mida butsu no
mite owasu nari
chiru sakura

amida buddha
is watching as they scatter,
those cherry blossoms

*19

82.

なむ〱と蛙も石に並びけり

namu namu to
kawazu mo ishi ni
narabi keri

i take refuge say
also the frogs on the rock
all sat in a row

*20

83.

のら猫が仏のひざを枕哉

nora neko ga
hotoke no hiza o
makura kana

a wandering cat
makes the lap of the buddha
into a pillow

84.

蝶が来てつれて行けり庭のてふ

chō ga kite
tsurete yuki keri
niwa no chō

a butterfly came
and then flew from the garden
with a butterfly

85.

出代やいづくも同じ梅の花

degawari ya
izuku mo onaji
ume no hana

the change of servants
no matter where it takes place,
the same plum blossom

*21

86.

ひたすらに咲うでもなし門の梅

hitasura ni
sakō de mo nashi
kado no ume

it does not appear
to try very hard to bloom,
that plum by the gate

87.

茶の煙柳と共にそよぐ也

cha no kemuri
yanagi to tomo ni
soyogu nari

the smoke from the tea
and the willow tree, they both
waver together

88.

人まねに鳩も雀も汐干かな

hitomane ni
hato mo suzume mo
shiohi kana

like people, pigeons
and sparrows down at ebb-tide
picking up shellfish

89.

天からでも降たるやうに桜哉

ten kara de mo
futtaru yō ni
sakura kana

they all rain down as if
they had fallen from heaven,
those cherry blossoms

90.

さくらくと唄れし老木哉

sakura sakura to
utaware shi
oigi kana

cherry blooms, cherry blossoms!
the song that was sung
of this ancient tree

91.

笠程な花が咲たぞとべ蛍

kasa hodona
hana ga sai ta zo
tobe hotaru

as large as a hat
is that flower which has bloomed,
fly there you firefly

92.

横乗の馬のつゞくや夕雲雀

yokonori no
uma no tsuzuku ya
yū-hibari

riders sat sideways,
horses passing one by one,
evening skylarks

93.

臭水の井戸の際より梅の花

kusa mizu no
ido no kiwa yori
ume no hana

alongside a well
that has foul-smelling water
a plum tree blossoms

94.

入相や桜のさはぐ鮎さわぐ

iriai ya
sakura no sawagu
ayu sawagu

at sunset bell's sound
cherry blossoms are clamouring,
trout also clamour

95.

人声にほつとしたやら夕桜

hitogoe ni
hotto shita yara
yū-zakura

with people's voices
at dusk, do cherry blossoms
feel pleased i wonder

96.

夕ざくらけふも昔に成にけり

yū-zakura
kyō mo mukashi ni
nari ni keri

evening cherries
in bloom today becoming
a thing of the past

97.

我庵や蛙初手から老を鳴く

waga io ya
kawazu shote kara
oi o naku

all around my hut
from the very first moment
frogs sang of old age

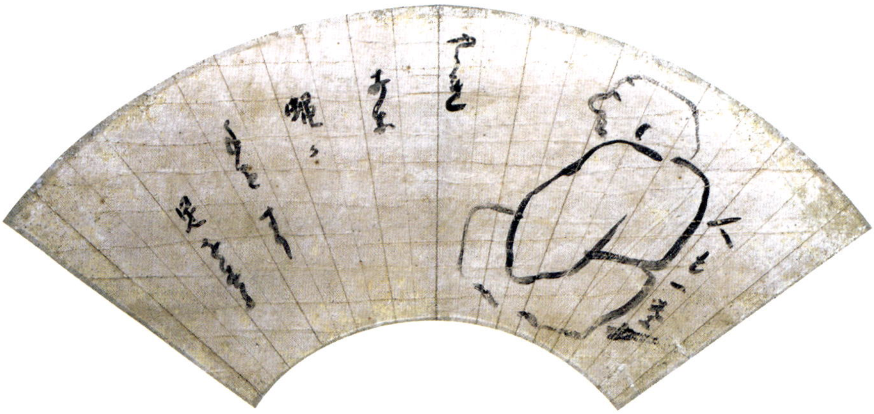

PLATE 6
Drawing and calligraphy by Issa,
Issa Memorial Hall. See haiku 98.

98.

やれ打な蝿が手をすり足をする

yare utsu na
hae ga te o suri
ashi o suru

do not kill that fly!
see the way that it wrings both
its hands and its feet

99.

涼風や力一ぱいきりぐす

suzukaze ya
chikara ippai
kirigirisu

in the breeze's cool
singing as hard as it can
a cricket is heard

100.

日盛りや葭雀に川の音もなき

hizakari ya
yoshikiri ni kawa no
oto mo naki

it is the midday
and reed warblers are in full song,
the river silent

101.

夕燕我には翌のあてもなし

yū-tsubame
ware ni wa asu no
ate mo nashi

evening swallow,
for me my tomorrow brings
no expectations

102.

朝涼や汁の実を釣るせどの海

asasuzu ya
shiru no mi o tsuru
sedo no umi

in the morning cool
he's fishing, to make some soup,
on the back door sea

103.

朝やけがよろこばしいか蝸牛

asayake ga
yorokobashii ka
katatsumuri

a red morning sky
is that making you happy
a snail as you are

*22

104.

這渡る橋の下より時鳥

haiwataru
hashi no shita yori
hototogisu

as i creep over
the hanging bridge, from below
it a cuckoo calls

105.

時鳥蝿虫めらもよっく聞け

hototogisu
hae mushi mera mo
yokku kike

the little cuckoo!
listen too you lowly flies
and you crawling worms

106.

涼風の曲りくねって来たりけり

suzukaze no
magari kunette
kitari keri

the cooling breezes
meandering on their way
have just now arrived

107.

涼しさや極楽浄土の這入口

suzushisa ya
gokuraku jōdo no
hairi-guchi

in summer coolness
the pure land of the utmost bliss
has an entrance way

*23

108.

あばれ蚤我手にかゝつて成仏せよ

abare-nomi
waga te ni kakatte
jōbutsu seyo

spirited, lively
flea, it will be by my hand
you'll become a buddha

109.

木の陰や蝶とやすむも他生の縁

ki no kage ya
chō to yasumu mo
tashō no en

in a tree's shadow
i rest with a butterfly friend
from an earlier life

110.

雲の峰いさゝか松が退くか

kumo no mine
isasaka matsu ga
shirizoku ka

under peaks of cloud
are the pine trees appearing
to shrink a little

111.

夕月や涼がてらの墓参

yūzuki ya
suzumi gatera no
haka-mairi

in the evening
moonlight they visit the graves,
enjoying the cool

112. 寝せつけし子のせんだくや夏の月

nesetsuke shi
ko no sendaku ya
natsu no tsuki

the child put to sleep,
she is washing the clothes now;
the moon of summer

113.

山の月花ぬす人をてらし給ふ

yama no tsuki
hana nusubito o
terashi tamō

over the mountains
the moon is shining kindly
on a flower thief

114.

狭くともいざ飛習へ庵の蚤

semaku tomo
iza tobinarae
io no nomi

although it is cramped
you must practise your jumping
you fleas in my hut

115.

年寄と見てや鳴蚊も耳のそば

toshiyori to
mite ya naku ka mo
mimi no soba

it must think me old
too, the mosquito that hums
so close to my ear

116. 閨の蚊のぶんとばかりに焼かれけり

neya no ka no
bun to bakari ni
yakare keri

a mosquito here
in the bedroom, just a hum
and it was burnt up

117.

是程のぼたんと仕かたする子哉

kore hodo no
botan to shikata
suru ko kana

the peony was
this big says the little girl
opening her arms

118.

蚤どもに松島見せて逃すぞよ

nomi domo ni
matsushima misete
nogasu zo yo

now all of you fleas
you'll be shown matsushima
and then you can go

*24

119.

石川や有明月と冷し瓜

ishi-kawa ya
ariake-zuki to
hiyashi uri

on a stream's pebbles
under the moon at daybreak
melons are cooling

120.

痩脛や涼めば虻に見込まるゝ

yase-zune ya
suzume ba abu ni
mikoma ruru

my very thin legs
were, as i was cooling down
checked by a horsefly

121.

蛍見の案内やするや庵の犬

hotaru mi no
anai ya suru ya
io no inu

for firefly viewing
to act as guide on the way
is the cottage dog

122.

しづかさや湖水の底の雲のみね

shizukasa ya
kosui no soko no
kumo no mine

such tranquility,
down in the depths of the lake
the peaks of the clouds

123.

水およぐ蚤の思ひや雲の峰

mizu oyogu
nomi no omoi ya
kumo no mine

the flea as it swims
is in hopes it will get to
the peaks of the clouds

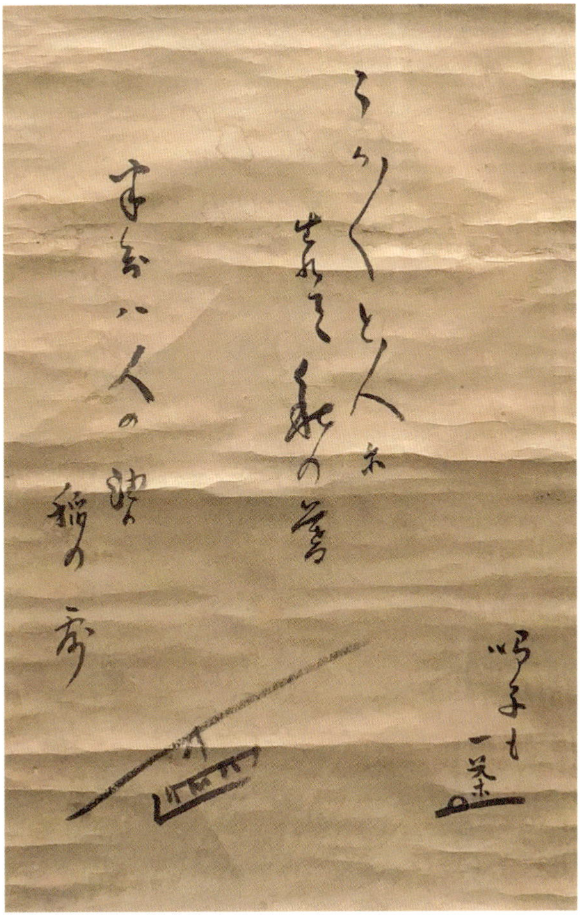

PLATE 7

Drawing and calligraphy by Issa,

Kobayashi Issa Museum. See haiku 124.

124.

うかうかと人に生れて秋の暮

uka uka to
hito ni umarete
aki no kure

carelessly without
thought being born a human,
autumn is ending

*25

125.

夜神楽や焚火の中へちる紅葉

yokagura ya
takibi no naka e
chiru momiji

shinto night dancing
and into the bonfires float
tinted, autumn leaves

*26

126.

玉霰夜たかは月に帰るめり

tama-arare
yotaka wa tsuki ni
kaeru meri

beautiful hailstones
are nighthawks now on their way
back up to the moon

*27

127.

うつくしやせうじの穴の天の川

utsukushi ya
shōji no ana no
ama no gawa

how lovely to see
through a torn paper window
the stream of heaven

*28

128.

寝返りをするぞ脇よれきりぐす

negaeri o
suru zo waki yore
kirigirisu

i'm turning over
so now you must move aside
you little cricket

129.

朝露に浄土参りのけいこ哉

asa tsuyu ni
jōdo mairi no
keiko kana

through morning dewdrops
the way to reach the pure land
is now being learnt

*29

130.

仏法がなくば光らじ草の露

buppō ga
naku ba hikara ji
kusa no tsuyu

without the dharma
there would be no glittering
dewdrops in the grass

*30

131.

御仏も笠きて立や辻踊

mihotoke mo
kasa kite tatsu ya
tsuji odori

even the buddha
stands in an umbrella hat
at the crossroads dance

*31

132.

かしましや江戸見た雁の帰り様

kashimashi ya
edo mita kari no
kaeri-zama

making a great noise,
wild geese who have seen edo
are coming back home

*32

133.

掃溜へ鶴の下りけり和歌の浦

hakidame e
tsuru no ori keri
wakanoura

to a rubbish pile
that's where a crane has just flown;
wakanoura!

*33

134.

蕣をふはりと浮す茶碗哉

asagao o
fuwari to ukasu
chawan kana

the morning glory
flower, it floats so gently
there in the teacup

135.

小言いふ相手は壁ぞ秋の暮

kogoto yū
aite wa kabe zo
aki no kure

to hear my complaints
there are only walls on this
autumn evening

136.

渋い所母が喰いけり山の柿

shibui toko
haha ga kui keri
yama no kaki

the astringent parts
are those that the mother ate,
mountain persimmons

137.

蓮の葉に此世の露は曲りけり

hasu no ha ni
kono yo no tsuyu wa
magari keri

on a lotus leaf
all this world's dewdrops are seen
to be distorted

138.

あきらめて子のない鹿は鳴ぬなり

akiramete
ko no nai shika wa
naka nu nari

giving it all up,
the deer without any fawns
calls for love no more

139.

風形に杖を月夜のかゞし哉

kazanari ni
tsue o tsukiyo no
kagashi kana

bent down by the wind
in the moonlight it leans on
a cane, this scarecrow

140.

淋しさを鶴に及すかゞし哉

sabishisa o
tsuru ni oyobosu
kagashi kana

passing loneliness
on to a crane is the work
of a scarecrow

141.

人に人かゞしにかゞし日の暮

hito ni hito
kagashi ni kagashi
hi no kururu

person by person
and scarecrow by scarecrow too,
the day is ending

PLATE 8
Drawing and calligraphy by Issa,
Kobayashi Issa Museum. See haiku 142.

142. さ越しかやゆひしてなめるけさの霜

saoshika ya
yuishite nameru
kesa no shimo

the deer are getting
together so as to lick
the frost this morning

143.

人のためしぐれておわす仏哉

hito no tame
shigurete owasu
hotoke kana

it is for our sake
enduring the winter rain,
that buddha figure

144.

とく暮よことしのやうな悪どしは

toku kure yo
kotoshi no yōna
aku-doshi wa

come to a quick end
oh year after having been
such a wicked one

145.

鳶ひよろひゝよろ神の御立げな

tobi hiyoro
hiiyoro kami no
otachi gena

hiyoro the kites
are crying, hiiyoro
as the gods set out

*34

146.

冷水にすゝり込だる天の川

hiya mizu ni
susuri kon daru
ama no gawa

in the cold water
i seem to be sipping stars
from heaven's river

*35

147.

蝸牛我と来て住め初時雨

katatsuburi
ware to kite sume
hatsu shigure

come on in you snail
and live together with me
in winter's first rain

148.

春待や子のない家ももちをつく

haru matsu ya
ko no nai ie mo
mochi o tsuku

waiting for new year
in even a childless house
they pound rice for cakes

149.

水仙や垣にゆい込むつくば山

suisen ya
kaki ni yuikomu
tsukubayama

the daffodils in
the fence hold in their embrace
mount tsukuba too

*36

150.

法の世は犬さへ十夜参哉

nori no yo wa
inu sae jūya
mairi kana

in this dharma world
even a dog goes into
the ten day retreat

*37

151.

雪の日や堂にぎっしり鳩雀

yuki no hi ya
dō ni gisshiri
hato suzume

on a snowy day
the temple's completely filled,
pigeons and sparrows

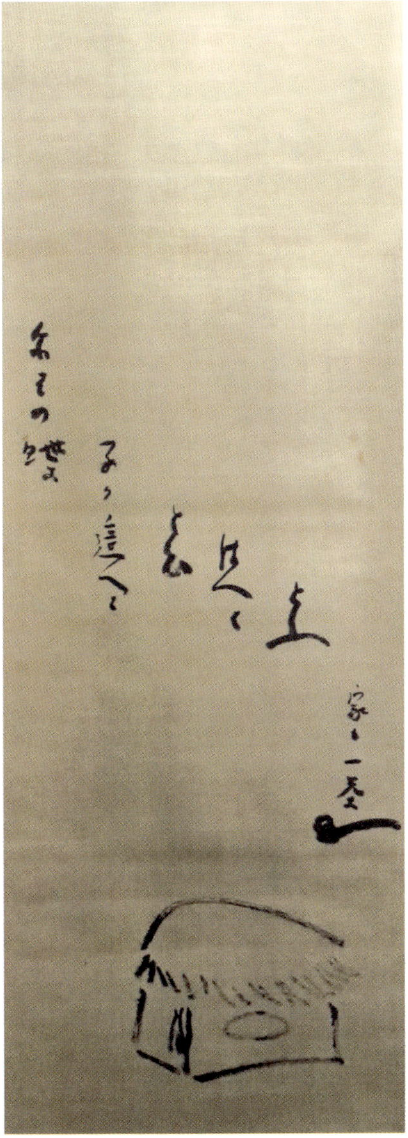

PLATE 9

Drawing and calligraphy by Issa,

Kobayashi Issa Museum. See haiku 152.

152. にはのてふ子が這へばとびはへばとぶ

niwa no chō
ko ga hae ba tobi
hae ba tobu

garden butterflies
when babies crawl after them
always fly away

153.

年玉や懐の子も手ゝをして

toshidama ya
futokoro no ko mo
tete o shite

the new year's presents,
the babe in the bosom too
holds out tiny hands

154.

元日やどちら向ても花の娑婆

ganjitsu ya
dochira mui temo
hana no shaba

it is new year's day,
in all directions are found
the blooms of this world

155.

一村は柳の中や春の雪

hito mura wa
yanagi no naka ya
haru no yuki

there in a hamlet
deep among willow trees
spring snow is falling

156.

御降や草の庵ももりはじめ

osagari ya
kusa no iori mo
mori hajime

the first rain this year
and with it there comes the first
leak in my thatched hut

157.

湯も浴て仏おがんで桜かな

yu mo abite
hotoke ogande
sakura kana

having bathed in hot
water and worshipped buddha,
the cherry blossoms!

158.

影ぼしもまめ息才でけさの春

kageboshi mo
mame sokusai de
kesa no haru

even my shadow
is safe and sound in good health
this morning in spring

159.

春雨や藪に吹るゝ捨手紙

harusame ya
yabu ni fuka ruru
sute-tegami

in the springtime rain
blown along through the thicket
there's a lost letter

160.

黄色組白組蝶の地どりけり

kiiro gumi
shiro gumi chō no
jidori keri

yellow swarms, white swarms
of butterflies have settled
their territories

161.

小食小屋富のおちけり春の雨

kojiki goya
tomi no ochi keri
haru no ame

on a beggar's hut
riches are showering down,
the rains in spring

162.

藪越の乞食笛よ鶯よ

yabu goshi no
kotsujiki bue yo
uguisu yo

adrift in the trees
the sound of the beggar's flute,
it's a bush warbler

163.

畠打や肱の先の鳰の海

hata uchi ya
kaina no saki no
nio no umi

as he plows his field,
only an arm's length away
a lake full of grebes

164.

かすむぞよ松が三本夫婦鶴

kasumu zo yo
matsu ga sanbon
meoto zuru

in the springtime mist
three pines and with them two cranes,
a husband and wife

165.

ゆうぜんとして山を見る蛙哉

yūzen to
shite yama o miru
kawazu kana

completely composed
as it gazes at mountains
a frog sitting there

166.

長閑さや浅间のけぶり昼の月

nodokasa ya
asama no keburi
hiru no tsuki

it is peacefulness
the smoke from mount asama
and a daytime moon

*38

167.

善光寺へ行て来た顔や雀の子

zenkōji e
itte kita kao ya
suzume no ko

it's back from zenkoji
that they appear to be coming
those sparrow children

*39

168. 気の毒やおれをしたふて来る小てふ

kinodoku ya
ore o shitōte
kuru kochō

it is sad that you
follow me with your love, you
who are butterflies

169.

川ほりや鳥なき里の飯時分

kawahori ya
tori naki sato no
meshi jibun

the bats fly over
a village that has no birds,
evening mealtime

170.

梅の花爰を盗めとさす月か

ume no hana
koko o nusume to
sasu tsuki ka

from the plum tree steal
this branch that is in full bloom
the moon seems to say

171.

身の上の鐘としりつゝ夕がすみ

mi no ue no
kane to shiri tsutsu
yū-gasumi

aware now the bell
is tolling my life away
in evening mist

172.

風雲ややけ野の火より日の暮るゝ

kazagumo ya
yakeno no hi yori
hi no kururu

under wind blown clouds
the fires of the burning fields
bring on the sunset

*40

173.

日の暮に凧の揃ふや町の空

hi no kure ni
tako no sorou ya
machi no sora

the sun going down
kites gathering in the sky
high over the town

174.

苦の娑婆やさくらが咲ばさいた迚

ku no shaba ya
sakura ga sake ba
sai ta tote

in this world of pain
there is still cherry blossom
that blooms even so

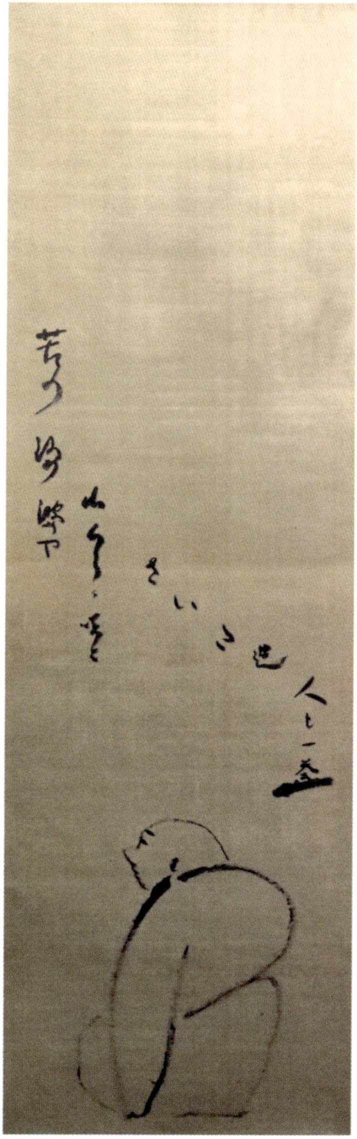

PLATE 10

Drawing and calligraphy by Issa,

Kobayashi Issa Museum. See haiku 174.

175.

庵の蛍瘦なくなりもせざりけり

io no hotaru
yase nakunari mo
se zari keri.

the firefly that lives
with me here in my hut, still
has not starved to death

176.

はつ蛍ついとそれたる手風哉

hatsu hotaru
tsui to sore taru
tekaze kana

the first firefly flew
up and away in the wind
i made with my hand

177.

涼しさや夜水のかゝる井戸の音

suzushisa ya
yomizu no kakaru
ido no oto

coolness in the night,
bathing water cascading
back into the well

178.

古郷や仏の顔のかたつむり

furusato ya
hotoke no kao no
katatsumuri

my own home village!
and the face of the buddha
is here in this snail

*41

179.

念仏の口からよばる蛍哉

nenbutsu no
kuchi kara yobaru
hotaru kana

nenbutsu said,
it is the same mouth that now
calls to the fireflies

*42

180.

昼の蚊を後にかくす仏かな

hiru no ka o
ushiro ni kakusu
hotoke kana

daytime mosquitoes
are hidden behind his back
by the buddha

181.

けしてよい時は来る也火取虫

keshite yoi
toki wa kuru nari
hitorimushi

putting out the light
was exactly the moment
the tiger moth came

182.

縁はなや二文花火も夜の体

en hana ya
nimon hanabi mo
yoru no tei

on the platform's edge
a handful of cheap fireworks
intensifies night

183.

長の日や沈香も焚かず屁もひらず

naga no hi ya
jinkō mo taka zu
he mo hira zu

it's been a long day
with there being no incense
and also no farts

184.

庵の蚤不便やいつか痩る也

io no nomi
fubin ya itsu ka
yaseru nari

the fleas in my hut
i feel so sorry for them
one day they'll get thin

185.

蓑虫の運の強さよ五月雨

minomushi no
un no tsuyosa yo
satsukiame

the bagworm insects
are so very fortunate
in the summer rain

*43

186.

せみなくやつくづく赤い風車

semi naku ya
tsukuzuku akai
kazaguruma

the cicadas' songs
sound just as thoroughly red
as paper windmills

*44

187.

けふの日も棒ふり虫よ翌も又

kyō no hi mo
bōfurimushi yo
asu no mata

today too was spent
on the mosquito larvae,
tomorrow again

188.

朝顔や人の顔にはそつがある

asagao ya
hito no kao ni wa
sotsu ga aru

the morning glories!
but in people's own faces
faults are to be found

*45

189.

大川へ虱とばする美人哉

ōkawa e
shirami tobasuru
bijin kana

out into the wide
river she's throwing her lice
that pretty woman

190.

入相の聞処なり草の華

iriai no
kiku tokoro nari
kusa no hana

at the very spot
where i heard the sundown bell
a weed in flower

191.

夏山や鶯雉ほとゝぎす

natsuyama ya
uguisu kigisu
hototogisu

in summer mountains
bush warblers' songs and pheasants
and lesser cuckoos

192.

先住のつけわたり也かんこ鳥

senjū no
tsukewatari nari
kankodori

after a former
dweller there's in succession
this mountain cuckoo

193.

しなのぢや上の上にも田うゑ唄

shinanoji ya
ue no ue ni mo
taue uta

on shinano road
higher and higher, i hear
the rice planters' song

*46

194.

旅人や野にさして行流れ苗

tabibito ya
no ni sashite yuku
nagare nae

a traveller plants
the rice stalks floating away
from a farmer's field

195.

山寺や縁の上なるしかの声

yamadera ya
en no ue naru
shika no koe

a mountain temple;
on the platform around it
the sound of a deer

196.

山水に米を搗かせて昼寝哉

yamamizu ni
kome o tsukasete
hirune kana

i leave the mountain
water still pounding the rice
while i take a nap

*47

197.

蜩やつい〳〵星の出やうに

higurashi ya
tsui-tsui hoshi no
deru yōni

cicadas trilling,
so suddenly suddenly
stars are appearing

198.

合点して蛍も寝るか夏花桶

gaten shite
hotaru mo neru ka
gebana oke

firefly, are you sure
you'll sleep here in that bucket
of summer flowers

199.

おゝさうじや迯るがかちぞはつ蛍

ō sō ja
niguru ga kachi zo
hatsu hotaru

it's certain, you first
firefly, the best way to win
is to fly away

*48

PLATE 11
Drawing and calligraphy by Issa,
Issa Memorial Hall. See haiku 199.

200.

有明や浅間の霧が膳をはふ

ariake ya
asama no kiri ga
zen o hau

at the break of day
mist from mount asama creeps
over the table

*49

201.

穂芒や細き心のさはがしき

ho-susuki ya
hosoki kokoro no
sawagashiki

the pampas grass plumes
uncontrollable tremors
of a lonely heart

202.

末の子や御墓参の箒持

sue no ko ya
ohaka mairi no
hōki-mochi

when visiting graves
the youngest child is the one
that carries the broom

203.

一つ消へ二つ消へつゝ灯籠哉

hitotsu kie
futatsu kie tsutsu
tōro kana

one of them goes out
and then two of them follow;
lanterns for the dead

204.

魂棚や上座して啼きりぎくす

tama-dana ya
jōza shite naku
kirigirisu

the bon festival;
high up there on the altar
a cricket in song

*50

205.

秋来ぬとしらぬ狗が仏かな

aki ki nu to
shira nu enoko ga
hotoke kana

the autumn has come,
the puppy not knowing it
it is a buddha

206.

鎌倉や今はかゞしの屋敷守

kamakura ya
ima wa kagashi no
yashiki mori

in kamakura
nowadays scarecrows behave
as the gatekeepers

*51

207.

かゞし立て餅なき家はなかりけり

kagashi tate
mochi naki ie wa
nakari keri

with the scarecrows about,
houses that have no rice cakes
are not to be found

208.

秋の夜や旅の男の針仕事

aki no yo ya
tabi no otoko no
hari-shigoto

autumn evening,
a traveller on his way
is sewing his clothes

209.

我星は年寄組や天の川

waga hoshi wa
toshiyori-gumi ya
ama no gawa

my star seems to be
there in a gang of old men,
river of heaven

*52

210.

乳呑子の風よけに立かゞし哉

chinomigo no
kazayoke ni tatsu
kagashi kana

a nursling is kept
from the wind by a scarecrow
standing behind it

211.

老の身やかゞしの前も恥しき

oi no mi ya
kagashi no mae mo
hazukashiki

now that i've grown old
even a scarecrow makes me
ashamed of myself

212.

夕暮や馬糞の手をも菊でふく

yūgure ya
maguso no te o mo
kiku de fuku

in the evening
wiping horse dung off their hands
with chrysanthemums

213.

船頭よ小便無用波の月

sendō yo
shōben muyō
nami no tsuki

now then you boatman
no peeing into the waves
where the moon shimmers

214.

夕暮の松見に来しをかへる雁

yūgure no
matsu mi ni ko shi o
kaeru kari

in the evening
after looking at pine trees
the geese are leaving

215.

今の世や役なし川も鳴子哉

ima no yo ya
yakunashi kawa mo
naruko kana

in the world of today
even a useless river
has a bird clapper

216.

山霧の足にからまる日暮哉

yama-giri no
ashi ni karamaru
higure kana

fog on the mountain
is swirling around my legs
as the sun goes down

217.

露の玉つまんだ時も仏哉

tsuyu no tama
tsuman da toki mo
hotoke kana

a dewdrop as i
picked it up had already
become a buddha

218.

秋霧や河原なでしこぱっと咲

aki-giri ya
kawara nadeshiko
patto saku

mist in the autumn
and pinks on the river beach
suddenly flowered

219.

名月や出家士諸商人

meigetsu ya
shukke samurai
sho akindo

in the harvest moon
there are monks and samurai
and sundry merchants

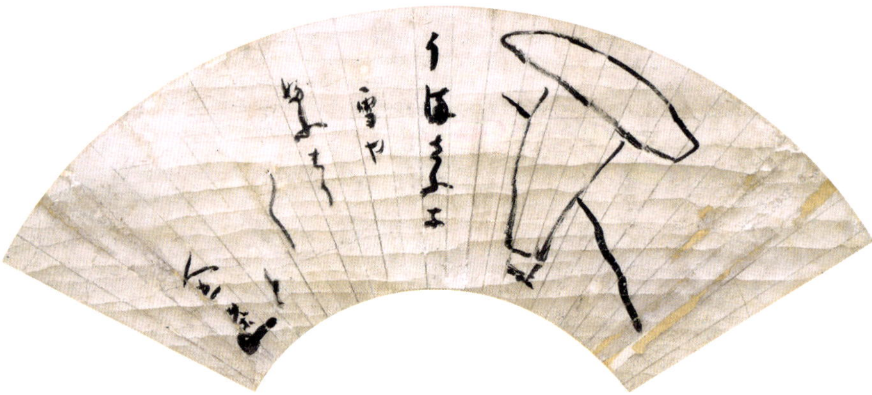

PLATE 12
Drawing and calligraphy by Issa,
Issa Memorial Hall. See haiku 220.

220.

うまさふな雪やふふはりくと

umasōna
yuki ya fūwari
fūwari to

it looks delicious
this snow that is coming down
softly so softly

221.

犬どもがよけてくれけり雪の道

inu domo ga
yokete kure keri
yuki no michi

dogs are politely
moving away to one side
of the snowy road

222.

大根引大根で道を教へけり

daiko-hiki
daiko de michi o
oshie keri

the radish puller
with a radish in his hand
is pointing the way

223.

母親を霜よけにして寝た子哉

haha oya o
shimo-yoke ni shite
neta ko kana

it is the mother
who serves to keep frost away
from her sleeping child

224.

御仲間に猫も坐とるや年わすれ

onakama ni
neko mo za toru ya
toshiwasure

as if one of us,
the cat is now seated here
as the year departs

225.

叱らるゝ人うらやまし年の暮

shikara ruru
hito urayamashi
toshi no kure

i am envious
of the child being scolded
at the year's ending

226.

掛取が土足ふみ込むいろり哉

kaketori ga
dosoku fumikomu
irori kana

the bill collector
steps in with his shoes still on
to get to the hearth

227.

のふなしはつみも又なし冬籠

nō nashi wa
tsumi mo mata nashi
fuyugomori

the good-for-nothing,
they also commit no crimes;
winter seclusion

228.

外は雪内は煤ふる栖かな

soto wa yuki
uchi wa susu furu
sumika kana

outside there is snow,
inside, the place where i live
is covered in soot

229.

夕月や御煤の過し善光寺

yūzuki ya
o-susu no sugi shi
zenkōji

an evening moon
when soot cleaning is over,
zenkoji temple

*53

230.

冬籠鳥料利にも念仏哉

fuyugomori
tori ryōri ni mo
nebutsu kana

winter seclusion;
when cooking a chicken too
nenbutsu wells up

*54

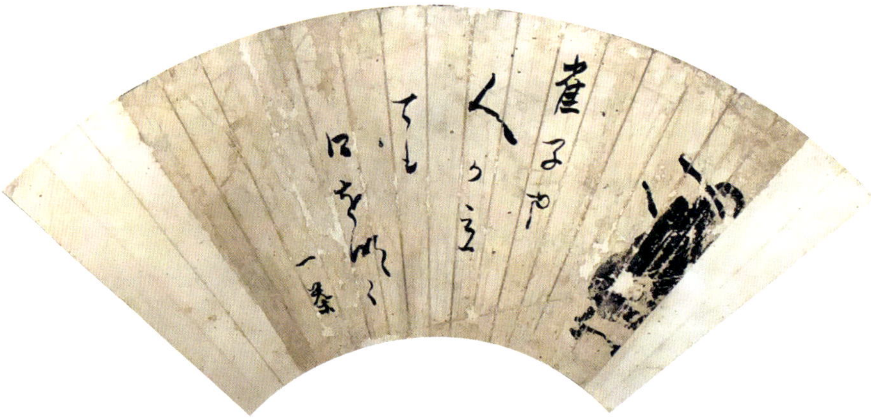

PLATE 13

Drawing and calligraphy by Issa,

Kobayashi Issa Museum. See haiku 231.

231.

雀子や人が立ても口を明く

suzumego ya
hito ga tatte mo
kuchi o aku

the baby sparrows
even when someone stands there
keep their mouths open

232.

ただ頼め花もはら〳〵あの通

tada tanome
hana mo hara hara
ano tōri

just entrust yourself,
do not petals flutter down
exactly like that

233.

世の中の梅よ柳よ人は春

yo no naka no
ume yo yanagi yo
hito wa haru

a world that is made
of plum blossoms and willows
is the people's spring

234.

天に雲雀人間海にあそぶ日ぞ

ten ni hibari
ningen umi ni
asobu hi zo

with the larks in the sky
and people down in the sea
it's a day of fun

235.

松間にひとりすまして梅の花

matsu ai ni
hitori sumashite
ume no hana

in among the pines
all by itself, a plum tree
comes into blossom

236.

白雲のかすみ吹抜く外山哉

shira kumo no
kasumi fukinuku
toyama kana

the white clouds now blow
through the mist on the mountain
close to the hamlet

237.

釣舟は花の上こぐ雲雀哉

tsuri-bune wa
hana no ue kogu
hibari kana

as a fishing boat's
being rowed through the blossom
a skylark is there

238.

きぬ〴〵やかすむ迄見る妹が家

kinuginu ya
kasumu made miru
imo ga ie

at lovers' parting
his eyes go back to her house
till there's only mist

239.

浅川や鍋すゝぐ手に春の月

asakawa ya
nabe susugu te ni
haru no tsuki

in the river shallows
over hands washing saucepans
there is a spring moon

240.

鶯や弥陀の浄土の東門

uguisu ya
mida no jōdo no
higashi-mon

a bush warbler sings,
in its song is the pure land's
easterly gateway

*55

241.

さく花や此世住居も今少

saku hana ya
kono yo zumai mo
ima sukoshi

blossoming flowers
too, only live in this world
for just a short time

242.

雨漏を何とおぼすぞ雛達

amamori o
nanto obosu zo
hiina tachi

rain is leaking in
so what do they think of it
now, those paper dolls

243.

月花や四十九年のむだ歩き

tsuki hana ya
shijūku nen no
muda aruki

the moon and blossoms,
forty-nine years of idle
wasteful wandering

244.

蝶とんで我身も塵のたぐひ哉

chō tonde
waga mi mo chiri no
tagui kana

butterflies flying
and i myself too, no more
than a kind of dust

245.

庵の梅よんどころなく咲にけり

io no ume
yondokoro naku
saki ni keri

my cottage plum tree!
there's no reason at all that
it came into bloom

246.

さをしかや蝶を振て又眠る

saoshika ya
chō o furutte
mata nemuru

after it's shaken
the butterflies off, the fawn
goes to sleep once more

247.

慈悲すれば糞をする也雀の子

jihi sure ba
hako o suru nari
suzume no ko

if you are loving
they will leave droppings on you
those baby sparrows

248.

母馬が番して呑す清水哉

haha-uma ga
ban shite nomasu
shimizu kana

its mother stands guard
on the foal as it's drinking
the limpid water

249.

菫咲川をとび越す美人哉

sumire saku
kawa o tobikosu
bijin kana

jumping a river
of violets in full bloom
a lovely woman

250.

としとへば片手出す子や更衣

toshi toe ba
katate dasu ko ya
koromogae

asked how old she is
her answer is five fingers
at the change of clothes

*56

251.

川縁や蝶を寝さする鍋の尻

kawaberi ya
chō o nesasuru
nabe no shiri

on the river bank
a butterfly goes to sleep
on a saucepan's back

252.

花は雲人はけぶりと成にけり

hana wa kumo
hito wa keburi to
nari ni keri

the blossoms have turned
into clouds, but the people
have just become smoke

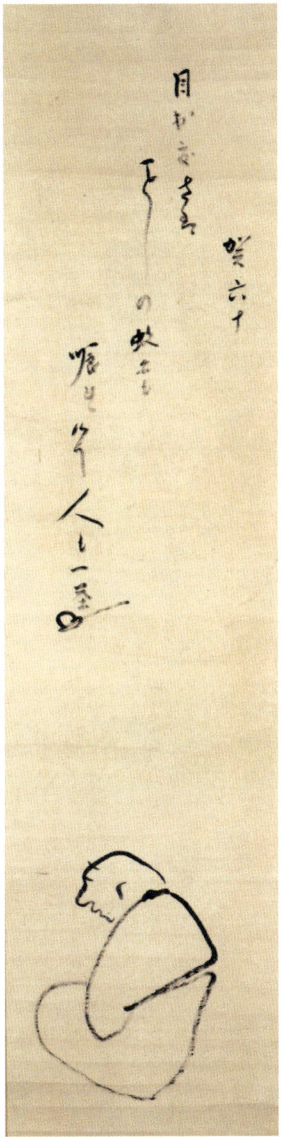

PLATE 14
Drawing and calligraphy by Issa,
Kakimori Bunko Foundation. See haiku 253.

253.

目出度さはことしの蚊にも喰はれけり

medetasa wa
kotoshi no ka ni mo
kuware keri

congratulate me!
by this year's mosquitoes i've
also been bitten

254.

前の世のおれがいとこか閑古鳥

saki no yo no
ore ga itoko ka
kankodori

in a former life
was it perhaps my cousin
that mountain cuckoo

255.

何もないが心安さよ涼しさよ

nani mo nai ga
kokoroyasusa yo
suzushisa yo

having no possessions
there's only this peacefulness
and the coolness too

256.

二つなき笠盗れし土用哉

futatsu naki
kasa nusuma re shi
doyō kana

it has been stolen,
my only woven rush hat
on the hottest day

257.

夕月や大肌ぬいでかたつむり

yūzuki ya
ōhada nuide
katatsumuri

in the evening
under the moon it is stripped
to the waist that snail

258.

風許りでも夕立の夕かな

kaze bakari
demo yūdachi no
yūbe kana

the wind by itself
foretells a sudden shower
by the evening

259.

夕立や裸で乗しはだか馬

yūdachi ya
hadaka de nori shi
hadaka-uma

a shower at dusk
makes me ride as if naked,
bareback on my horse

260.

縁の蝿手をする所を打れけり

en no hae
te o suru tokoro o
utare keri

out on the platform
while rubbing its hands together
a fly got swatted

261.

かくれ家や手追ひ蛍の走入

kakurega ya
teoi hotaru no
hashiri iru

a secluded house,
so a firefly that's wounded
rushes to enter

262.

人来たら蛙となれよ冷し瓜

hito kitara
kawazu to nare yo
hiyashi uri

if anyone comes
transform yourselves into frogs
you cooling melons

263.

蠅打に花さく草も打れけり

hae-uchi ni
hana saku kusa mo
utare keri

with a fly swatter
a blossoming wild flower
also got swatted

264. 手をすりて蚊屋の小すみを借りにけり

te o surite
kaya no kosumi o
kari ni keri

rubbing hands, it used
a tiny mosquito net
corner for a nap

265.

蚤の迹かぞへながらに添乳哉

nomi no ato
kazoe nagara ni
soeji kana

the bites of the fleas
added up by a mother
breast-feeding in bed

266.

もたいなや昼寝して聞田うへ唄

mottaina ya
hirune shite kiku
taue-uta

i am somewhat ashamed
when taking a nap, to hear
the rice planters' songs

267.

けし提て群集の中を通りけり

keshi sagete
gunshū no naka o
tōri keri

he carries poppies
along in his hand as he makes
his way through the crowd

268.

夕顔の花で涕かむおばゝ哉

yūgao no
hana de hana kamu
obaba kana

the moonflower made
her blow her nose into it,
that ancient woman

269.

さし柳螢とぶ夜と成にけり

sashi-yanagi
hotaru tobu yo to
nari ni keri

with the willow grown
from a cutting the fireflies
now fly there at night

270.

とぶ蛍女の髪につながれな

tobu hotaru
onna no kami ni
tsunagare na

firefly as you fly
don't get yourself tangled up
in a woman's hair

271.

山国やあるが上にも雲の峰

yama-guni ya
aru ga ue ni mo
kumo no mine

in mountain country
far up above it there rise
the peaks of the clouds

272.

これでこそ御時鳥松に月

kore de koso
on hototogisu
matsu ni tsuki

it is wonderful
the sound of a cuckoo's call
with moon in the pines

273.

無常鐘蠅虫めらもよっくきけ

mujō-gane
hae mushi mera mo
yokku kike

bell of transience,
all of you flies and worms too
listen with great care

274.

魚どもは桶としらでや夕涼

uo domo wa
oke to shira de ya
yūsuzumi

the fish seem to be
unaware of the bucket
in evening cool

275.

時鳥火宅の人を笑らん

hototogisu
kataku no hito o
warō ran

the lesser cuckoo,
are those in the burning house
what it laughs at now

*57

PLATE 15

Drawing and calligraphy by Issa,

Kobayashi Issa Museum. See haiku 276.

276.

名月の御覧の通り屑家哉

meigetsu no
goran no tōri
kuzuya kana

lit by the bright moon
it's seen for just what it is,
a rubbishy house

277.

白露に浄土参りのけいこ哉

shira tsuyu ni
jōdo mairi no
keiko kana

from the white dewdrops
how to get to the pure land
is what can be learned

*58

278.

虫なくやきのふは見へぬ壁の穴

mushi naku ya
kinō wa mienu
kabe no ana

insects are singing,
i could not yesterday see
that hole in the wall

279.

古犬や蚯蚓の唄にかんじ顔

furu inu ya
mimizu no uta ni
kanji gao

to the aged dog
the song that the earthworms sing
appears impressive

*59

280.

山は虹いまだに湖水は野分哉

yama wa niji
imada ni kosui wa
nowaki kana

over the mountain
there's a rainbow, yet on the lake
an autumn gale blows

281.

世の中や鳴虫にさい上づ下手

yo no naka ya
naku mushi ni sai
jōzu heta

in the world at large
even some insects sing well
and others badly

282.

さをしかの喰こぼしけり萩の花

saoshika no
kui koboshi keri
hagi no hana

a young deer has been
eating, scattering petals
from the bush clovers

283.

売馬の親かへり見る秋の雨

uri uma no
oya kaeri miru
aki no ame

the pony that's sold
still looks back at its mother
in the autumn rain

284.

菊さくや馬糞山も一けしき

kiku saku ya
maguso yama mo
hito keshiki

chrysanthemum blooms
and a heap of horse dung
produce a fine sight

285.

紫の雲にいつ乗るにしの海

murasaki no
kumo ni itsu noru
nishi no umi

on the purpling clouds
when will i be setting sail;
the sea in the west

286.

名月にけろりと立しかゞし哉

meigetsu ni
kerori to tachi shi
kagashi kana

a brilliant moon;
of no concern to scarecrows
that are standing there

287.

人はいさ直な案山子もなかりけり

hito wa isa
suguna kagashi mo
nakari keri

perhaps like people,
a scarecrow that is upright
is not to be found

288.

稲妻や狗ばかり無欲顔

inazuma ya
enokoro bakari
muyoku gao

a flash of lightning
and only the puppy's face
seems not to worry

289.

木つゝきや一ツ所に日の暮るゝ

kitsutsuki ya
hitotsu tokoro ni
hi no kururu

as a woodpecker
keeps on and on in one place
the day is ending

290.

露ちるやむさい此世に用なしと

tsuyu chiru ya
musai kono yo ni
yō nashi to

the dewdrops scatter
declaring they're finished
with this defiled world

291.

行秋を尾花がさらば〱哉

yuku aki o
obana ga saraba
saraba kana

waving in autumn
pampas grasses are saying
goodbye and goodbye

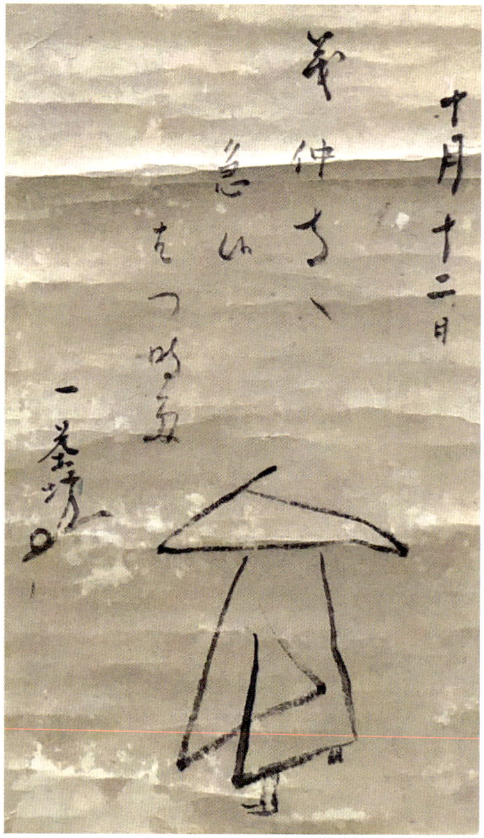

PLATE 16
Drawing and calligraphy by Issa,
Kobayashi Issa Museum. See haiku 292.

292.

義仲寺へいそぎ候はつしぐれ

gichūji e
isogi sōrō
hatsu shigure

it's to gichuji
i'm hurrying on my way
in winter's first rain

*60

293.

仏ともならでうか〱老の松

hotoke to mo
narade uka uka
oi no matsu

not yet a buddha
and just idling on and on
is this ancient pine

294.

散芒寒くなるのが目に見ゆる

chiru susuki
samuku naru no ga
me ni miyuru

falling pampas grass
lets one see with one's own eyes
the increasing cold

295.

木がらしや塒に迷ふ夕烏

kogarashi ya
negura ni mayou
yū-garasu

in the winter wind
he can't find a place to roost,
that evening crow

296.

炭の火や齢のへるもあの通り

sumi no hi ya
yowai no heru mo
ano tōri

like a charcoal fire
the remaining years of life
die down the same way

297.

我星はどこに旅寝や天の川

waga hoshi wa
doko ni tabine ya
ama no gawa

where will my own star
be stopping now for the night,
river of heaven

*61

298.

死んだならおれが日を鳴閑古鳥

shin da nara
ore ga hi o nake
kankodori

when i come to die
sing your song on my death day
you mountain cuckoo

*62

299.

大雪やおれが真上の天の川

ōyuki ya
ore ga ma ue no
ama no gawa

a heavy snowfall
and there right over my head
is heaven's river

*63

300.

是がまあつひの栖か雪五尺

kore ga maa
tsui no sumika ka
yuki go shaku

now, here it has come,
will it be my final home
this five feet of snow

*64

TAILPIECE

Issa portrait by Shunpo, one of his disciples,

Issa Memorial Hall.

Notes

1. Mount Higashiyama overlooks eastern Kyoto and its dark form would remain visible on clear spring nights.

2. Mount Asama, just under 8,500 ft high, is a striking, complex volcano about 90 miles northwest of Tokyo on the border of Nagano prefecture and still the most active on Honshu, Japan's main island, last erupting in 2015.

3. This is a reference to Kannon Bodhisattva, or Avalokitêśvara. This bodhisattva of love and compassion, often depicted in female form and known as the Goddess of Mercy, was extremely popular and her image was worshipped in various forms in many shrines and temples.

4. Zenkoji in Nagano, about 240 miles northwest of Tokyo, close to Issa's birthplace in Kashiwabara, was founded in the seventh century and was notable for being run, not by a single sect, but in close cooperation by the Tendai and Jōdoshū schools, associated with Shinshū and other Buddhist sects. It was the subject of a famous haiku by Matsuo Basho.

5. In Pure Land Buddhism the *nenbutsu* (see note 7 below) is pronouncing the name of Amida Buddha, *namuamidabutsu,* and an expression of joy and gratitude for all that he has done through his Original Vow.

6. Issa was born in Kashiwabara, then a small village close to Nagano, from which the present prefecture, formerly the province of Shinano, takes its name.

7. This refers to Amida Buddha's Pure Land of Bliss, which was generally thought of as being far out to the west beyond the setting sun. It is reached by the recital of the *nenbutsu* (see note 5 above) with absolute faith in Amida Buddha's Original Vow to save all sentient beings.

8. For *namuamidabutsu*, "I take refuge in Amida Buddha," see note 5 above.

9. Mount Kamiji, itself revered as a holy mountain, is close to the Grand Shrine at Ise in central Honshu near the city of Mie and the most important of all the Shinto shrines in Japan.

10. Sumida River is a branch of the Arakawa and flows through Tokyo into Tokyo bay.

11. For Mount Asama, see note 2 above.

12. This haiku was written when Issa was visiting the grave of his daughter, Sato, on the 35th day after her death.

13. Although butterflies are marker words for spring, this one is flying in the autumn wind, hence its placement in that season. In haiku no. 52 this was immediately obvious as autumn was referred to in the first five syllables.

14. Wakanoura, on the coast about 240 miles south-west of Tokyo, was renowned for its inspiring natural beauty, but Issa's attention was caught by the fact that what attracted these no less magnificent birds was its rubbish dump. Haiku no. 133 below refers to another crane doing the same thing.

15. Miidera is a huge temple complex and pilgrimage focus in Otsu, the main port on Lake Biwa at the foot of Mount Hiei, where the great Tendai Buddhist centre is situated.

16. This refers to the fact that in Issa's day eyebrows were often shaved and replaced with smudges on the forehead made with soot, a practice now generally confined to theatrical performances such as Noh plays.

17. The Ten Day Retreat for silent meditation by Pure Land Buddhists was held in November, the tenth month in the lunar calendar.

18. See Plate 5. This refers to the haiku on the left of the fan; that on the right reads *hoku hoku to / kasunde kuru wa / donata kana.*

19. Amida Buddha and his Original Vow to save all sentient beings is the central focus of Shin Buddhism.

20. See notes 8 and 5 above.

21. The annual cycle of activities in Japan was tightly organised in accordance with strictly observed traditions and tied to specific dates, in this case involving the change of servants on 5th March.

22. 'Red sky at night, shepherd's delight, red sky in the morning, shepherd's warning', with its presage of rain in a matter of hours, is the English proverbial equivalent of what Issa has in mind, and it is interesting to see the extent to which similar meteorological events across the world, such as the passage of warm fronts, give rise, in widely separated communities and widely differing languages, to similar folk wisdom and sayings.

23. For the Pure Land, see note 7 above.

24. Matsushima Bay on the east coast of Honshu, just over 230 miles north of Tokyo, is one of the most fabled beauty spots in Japan, with some 260 wooded islands of varying sizes.

25. See Plate 7 above. This refers to the haiku on the right; that on the left reads *hanbun wa / hito no abura ka / ine no tsuyu.*

26. This refers to a traditional form of sacred folk dancing in honour of the kami.

27. 'Nighthawks' was the term for the lowest form of prostitute, but Issa saw the beauty in them.

28. River or Stream of Heaven is the far more poetic Japanese term for the Milky Way.

29. For the Pure Land, see note 7 above.

30. The Dharma has many meanings, including truth, the structure of reality, or the teachings and practices set out by the Buddha. Along with the Buddha and the Sangha, it is one of the Three Jewels or refuges through which liberation is attained.

31. This probably refers to one of the hats made with woven reeds or slats of bamboo and commonly used by peasants and others to shield themselves from the rain.

32. Edo was the capital city of Japan during the Tokugawa Shogunate from 1603 to 1867, and was renamed Tokyo at the time of the Meiji Restoration in 1868.

33. For Wakanoura, see note 14 above.

34. This refers to the departure of the gods or *kami* for their annual gathering, in October according to the lunar calendar, at the great Shinto shrine at Izumo on the island of Honshu, close to the Japan Sea.

35. This, as is mentioned in the Introduction, is a classic example of Issa's ability, despite what might well seem at times to be an overwhelming interest in the seemingly trivial details of the natural world, to make them reach out to the stars; to make so few words do so much.

36. Mount Tsukuba is a famous mountain with twin peaks, 60 miles north-east of Tokyo.

37. For Dharma, see note 30 above, and for the Ten Day Retreat, note 17 above.

38. For Mount Asama, see note 2 above.

39. For Zenkoji, see note 4 above.

40. This refers, not to the crematoria associated with the Bon Festival of remembrance for dead ancestors, whose spirits return for a short time, held in the autumn, but to preparing fields for cultivation in the spring.

41. For home village, see note 6 above.

42. For the *nenbutsu*, see note 5 above.

43. Bagworm insects spend part of their life cycle protected from the rain in a hard cocoon suspended from a twig.

44. Issa's poems are much less often characterised than those of Matsuo Basho by observations giving the effect of what is now called synaesthesia (see Introduction, page 11 above) in which stimulation of one of the senses is accompanied by involuntary experiences in another, but this particular haiku involves an extreme example of it, two sounds from completely different sources, one of them organic and the other inorganic, being seen as red.

45. This haiku depends on the fact that morning glories are called 'morning faces' in Japanese.

46. Shinano is an old province of Japan that is now Nagano Prefecture. Shinano was a large area bordering on many provinces.

47. Pounding rice to remove the bran was generally carried out using the feet, but where sufficient fast-flowing water was available, water mills, such as the one that Issa was tending, could be constructed to do the work mechanically.

48. This haiku is on the right; that on the left reads *shitaya ichiban / no kao shite / koromogae.*

49. For Mount Asama, see note 2 above.

50. The Bon Festival in honour of the ancestral spirits, who return for a short time, is still held in July or August in Japan, but in Issa's day would have been held in the seventh month, which is autumn in the lunar calendar.

51. Kamakura, on the coast 27 miles south of Tokyo, is a major Buddhist centre famous for its great, 37 ft high, bronze Buddha of 1252, originally covered in gold leaf, which can be entered to see the details of its construction out of many separate plates of metal.

52. For River of Heaven, see note 28 above.

53. For Zenkoji, see note 4 above.

54. For the *nenbutsu*, see note 5 above.

55. For the Pure Land, see note 7 above.

56. In Japan, as was mentioned in note 21 above, the seasons were very strictly defined and annual activities tended to be assigned to particular days of the year and carried out in unison, the 'change of clothes' between spring and summer and between summer and autumn, to take account of changing temperatures, being set for the first days of the fourth and tenth months in the lunar calendar, which refer to May and November in the solar calendar.

57. This haiku refers to the famous parable in the *Lotus Sutra* in which a family of children go on playing heedlessly in a burning house.

58. For the Pure Land, see note 7 above.

59. As earthworms don't sing, it has been suggested that what the dog was listening to was a mole cricket.

60. Gichuji, a small temple in the village of Zeze, near Otsu, some 365 miles from Tokyo on the shores of Lake Biwa, the largest lake in Japan, houses the tomb of Matsuo Basho, the great haiku poet and forerunner of Buson and Issa.

61. For River of Heaven, see note 28 above.

62. Since Japanese mountain cuckoos are migratory and winter in the south, it was not possible for Issa's wish to be fulfilled, as he died in midwinter, but the cuckoo could have sung for him after its return in the following spring.

63. For River of Heaven, see note 28 above.

64. There may have been an element of premonition in this haiku, which Issa wrote in 1812, some two years after he had finally returned to his home village in an area noted for its heavy winter snowfalls. He eventually died on the 5th of January 1828, and what came to be viewed as being his death verse was carved on his tombstone.

Index of First Lines and Illustrations

FRONTISPIECE

Introduction

PLATE 1

PLATE 2

samidare no	in the summer rains,	21
yabu-mura ya	in a poor hamlet	22
suzukaze no	the breeze's coolness	23
meshi keburi	the rice cooking smoke	24
yo ga yoku ba	as all now goes well	25
hatsu hotaru	the first firefly, as	26
ari no michi	this pathway for ants,	27
chonbori to	a minuscule thing	28
shiba no to ya	for a brushwood gate	29
waga yado wa	here in my cottage,	30
nigeru nari	as they run away	31
nomi kan da	when cracking a flea	32
yoigoshi no	tofu makers' lights	33
nomi domo ga	for all of you fleas	34
suzushisa wa	how cool it now is;	35
onozukara	of its own accord	36
tobu na nomi	flea, don't ever jump	37
tetsudatte	I need to have help	38
matsu no semi	pine tree cicadas	39
matsu chiru ya	pines shed their needles;	40
mi no ue no	unaware the bell	41
suzukaze no	how many gateways	42
iriai no	the setting sun bell	43
ame mi tsubu	just three drops of rain	44
koromogae	a new summer robe	45

PLATE 3

kōshite wa	to live here like this	46
kari yo kari	wild goose, wild goose there,	47
kaeru kari	wild geese on your way	48
tōyama ga	the distant mountains	49
akikaze ya	in the autumn breeze	50

yūzuki ya — in the evening — 111
nesetsuke shi — the child put to sleep, — 112
yama no tsuki — over the mountains — 113
semaku tomo — although it is cramped — 114
toshiyori to — it must think me old — 115
neya no ka no — a mosquito here — 116
kore hodo no — the peony was — 117
nomi domo ni — now all of you fleas — 118
ishi-kawa ya — on a stream's pebbles — 119
yase-zune ya — my very thin legs — 120
hotaru mi no — for firefly viewing — 121
shizukasa ya — such tranquility, — 122
mizu oyogu — the flea as it swims — 123

PLATE 7

uka uka to — carelessly without — 124
yokagura ya — shinto night dancing — 125
tama-arare — beautiful hailstones — 126
utsukushi ya — how lovely to see — 127
negaeri o — i'm turning over — 128
asa tsuyu ni — through morning dewdrops — 129
buppō ga — without the dharma — 130
mihotoke mo — even the buddha — 131
kashimashi ya — making a great noise, — 132
hakidame e — to a rubbish pile — 133
asagao o — the morning glory — 134
kogoto yū — to hear my complaints — 135
shibui toko — the astringent parts — 136
hasu no ha ni — on a lotus leaf — 137
akiramete — giving it all up, — 138
kazanari ni — bent down by the wind — 139
sabishisa o — passing loneliness — 140
hito ni hito — person by person — 141

PLATE 8

PLATE 9

kazagumo ya	under wind blown clouds	172
hi no kure ni	the sun going down	173
ku no shaba ya	in this world of pain	174

PLATE 10

io no hotaru	the firefly that lives	175
hatsu hotaru	the first firefly flew	176
suzushisa ya	coolness in the night,	177
furusato ya	my own home village!	178
nenbutsu no	nenbutsu said,	179
hiru no ka o	daytime mosquitoes	180
keshite yoi	putting out the light	181
en hana ya	on the platform's edge	182
naga no hi ya	it's been a long day	183
io no nomi	the fleas in my hut	184
minomushi no	the bagworm insects	185
semi naku ya	the cicadas' songs	186
kyō no hi mo	today too was spent	187
asagao ya	the morning glories!	188
ōkawa e	out into the wide	189
iriai no	at the very spot	190
natsuyama ya	in summer mountains	191
senjū no	after a former	192
shinanoji ya	on shinano road	193
tabibito ya	a traveller plants	194
yamadera ya	a mountain temple;	195
yamamizu ni	i leave the mountain	196
higurashi ya	cicadas trilling,	197
gaten shite	firefly, are you sure	198
ō sō ja	it's certain, you first	199

PLATE 11

PLATE 13

PLATE 14